The
Montessori
Toddler
Activity Book

THE
MONTESSORI
Toddler
Activity Book

60 AT-HOME GAMES AND ACTIVITIES FOR CURIOUS TODDLERS

BETH WOOD

Illustrated by Denise Holmes

ROCKRIDGE PRESS

Interior and Cover Designer: Tricia Jang
Art Producer: Meg Baggott
Editor: Laura Bryn Sisson
Production Editor: Nora Milman
Production Manager: Jose Olivera

Illustrations © 2021 Denise Holmes. Illustrator portrait courtesy of Tara Vorhes.

ISBN: Print 978-1-64876-920-7 | eBook 978-1-64876-263-5
R0

THIS BOOK IS DEDICATED
TO ANTHONY AND QUENTIN
AND TO ALL THE CHILDREN
I HAVE HELD TREASURES
FOR IN MY POCKETS.

CONTENTS

INTRODUCTION VIII

Part 1: Montessori and Your Toddler 1

CHAPTER 1:
Raising a Toddler the Montessori Way 3

CHAPTER 2:
Activities the Montessori Way 11

Part 2: Montessori Activities 17

CHAPTER 3:
Let's Move:
Activities for Motor Skills 19

CHAPTER 4:
Art Is for All 33

CHAPTER 5:
A Day in the Life:
Activities for Practical Life 47

CHAPTER 6:
The Five Senses:
Activities for Sensory Stimulation 61

CHAPTER 7:
Fun with Language:
Activities for Language Development 75

RESOURCES 88   REFERENCES 89   INDEX 90

INTRODUCTION

HELLO, EVERYONE! My name is Beth, and I'm an accredited Montessori Guide for 0- to 3- and 3- to 6-year-olds and an accredited Montessori Assistant for 6- to 12-year-olds. I'm also a Montessori educational consultant, helping schools and families incorporate more authentic practices of the Montessori Method into their days.

Montessori "found" me when our oldest son (now 20) was 3 years old and we were looking for a different way of schooling, something more than traditional education. Its child-centered, scientifically based, holistic way of engaging with children immediately drew me in and I fell in love with it. It found me again when our youngest was born prematurely, and we wanted the best way to support his natural development at home.

This book is what I wish I had as a parent of a toddler! It's a book you can keep close at hand to help fill your days with peaceful, purposeful, Montessori-compatible toddler activities easily done at home no matter where you live.

Some of the most important social-emotional and neurological developments in a child's life happen during the years of toddlerhood, between the ages of 1 and 3. With the Montessori Method, we create intentionally prepared environments to meet children's developmental needs holistically.

> We see the figure of the child who stands before us with [their] arms held open, beckoning humanity to follow.
>
> —DR. MARIA MONTESSORI

That's what this book can help you with!

I've broken this book into two parts. Part 1 includes helpful information about the Montessori Method, a toddler's social-emotional and neurological development, and how to use the following activities.

In part 2, I've gathered 60 of my favorite toddler-specific Montessori-compatible activities. These activities are divided into five core areas of learning: motor skills, art, daily or practical life, sensory stimulation, and language. Each easy-to-follow activity focuses on a specific developmental skill and offers caregivers clear instructions on how to prepare and carry out the activities in the Montessori way, to empower their toddler's independence and discovery, ultimately building their self-confidence and resilience. The activities in this book are designed to help you quickly and easily prepare beautiful learning moments in your toddler's day, where they can safely and effectively build their curiosity and self-reliance while having a lot of fun.

LET'S BEGIN OUR JOURNEY TOGETHER!

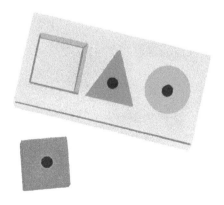

A child is both
a hope and a promise
for all [human] kind.

—DR. MARIA MONTESSORI

Montessori and Your Toddler

The years of toddlerhood are some of the most important in a child's life. In part 1 of this book, you will learn about the gentle, peaceful principles of the Montessori Method and how it can aid a child's unfolding development naturally. You'll learn how to prepare for the 60 Montessori-style activities and bring the world of Montessori to your toddler.

The child's development follows a path of successive stages of independence, and our knowledge of this must guide us in our behavior towards [them].

—DR. MARIA MONTESSORI

RAISING A TODDLER THE MONTESSORI WAY

In chapter 1, we'll review what the Montessori Method is and specifically how it helps children ages 1 to 3. We'll also dive deeper into the development of the 1- to 3-year-old age group to examine how raising a toddler using Montessori is, in some ways, different than traditional methods. Lastly, I'll share the practical benefits you can gain from raising a Montessori toddler and how using the fun and easy activities in this book can help you do just that!

THE BASICS OF MONTESSORI

The Montessori Method is a beautiful and gentle way of helping every child reach their full and amazing potential. It can inspire that flame of imagination and spark a love of learning that will last a lifetime. A toddler's busy day can be calmed and made more peaceful simply by implementing some basic Montessori principles, such as routines, a simple child-size prepared environment, and freedom within limits. This peaceful way of being with children is one of the main reasons I fell in love with this approach years ago. It is the original "gentle parenting" method that puts the child at its center.

Dr. Maria Montessori created this method of education more than 100 years ago to change how adults look at educating children. Dr. Montessori carefully observed and documented how children learn, and from her years of observations and experiments with her first schools, this amazing method was born.

In child-led learning, the child is the leader of their knowledge. The child has curiosity and quests for knowledge. The adult is not the teacher, but rather the preparer of the environment that will teach the child. The environment is prepared so specifically partly because learning objectives are hands-on. Instead of an adult imparting knowledge on a child, the child experiments using their own hands and senses to discover that which they are interested in. Also, the environment is prepared for the child to have as much independence as possible. Social neurological research shows that when a person independently accomplishes something, they are much more likely to retain that information with a greater sense of self-worth and self-confidence. Building strong independence skills early helps children become more independent later in life. Finally, Dr. Montessori believed that education has a responsibility toward promoting world peace and social justice. Peace Education is the purposeful work toward anti-biased, anti-racist education from birth.

The Montessori Method has spread around the world to 22,000 Montessori schools and countless homes. Many families have experienced firsthand how this learning method has helped their children become better prepared for what the future holds. Children learning under the Montessori Method are often better at understanding abstract academic concepts and have much more social-emotional intelligence at a younger age.

The positive benefits of this method are not just for the school-age child, but for toddlers as well. Dr. Montessori found that by preparing an engaging environment with purposeful activities and implementing the basic principles of her method, families can help their toddlers reach their full potential.

We know that toddlers are busy! They love to do things for themselves. They also love to experiment with the world around them, trying new things, taking chances, and making sense of the world. This exciting time in their lives is a time when their language is exploding, and they love exploring all that the world has to offer. It can also be a time when families are seeking new ways of engaging their children, wondering how to more purposefully interact with them and how to help them navigate the big emotions that come with the toddler years.

Through Montessori, we can provide toddlers unique opportunities to strengthen their independence and love of learning. We can be active participants in their discovery of all that this amazing world has to offer, and we can help set them up for a lifetime love of learning!

These amazing benefits for your toddler can all be achieved by preparing simple and easy activities in the home that focus on some important Montessori-Method key concepts. Let's review some of these now.

The Prepared Environment

The Montessori prepared environment is the most important aspect of the Montessori approach. It can include all parts of the home and fosters a child's independence and love of learning. A carefully prepared space should be easy to physically move in and have developmentally appropriate materials, laid out in an accessible way to allow maximum independence and in a way that does not overwhelm the child. This could include a mirror at a toddler's height to help children be independent in body care and a child-size chair in a bedroom to help children put on clothes by allowing them to sit. The prepared environment also includes the adult, who needs to be prepared to observe and interact with the child.

Observe and Guide

Observation is the key to successfully implementing the Montessori Method. The adult observes the child in the environment and how they interact with the activities and the overall experience. Based on those observations, the adult guides the child to try new things independently and adjusts the prepared environment as needed.

The Absorbent Mind

This is the Montessori term for a young child's endless natural curiosity and ability to effortlessly learn concepts. They do this simply by listening to or observing their environment. The fostering of the absorbent mind builds the foundation for strong self-confidence and independence in the child.

A Child's Freedom within Limits

A child's freedom in the prepared environment is important! They choose what activity they use and how long to use it. Our observations help change and limit the prepared environment. If your toddler has shown they're not yet ready for something, remove it from the environment and replace it with something developmentally appropriate.

Sensitive Periods

This is the Montessori term for the intense interest periods that a child passes through. Montessori identified 11 different Sensitive Periods occurring from birth through the age of 6. We will address these four Sensitive Periods most relevant for ages 1 to 3:

★ The Sensitive Period for Order is the intense need for consistency and repetition.

★ The Sensitive Period for Movement is the need to move one's body in intentional, new, different, or challenging ways.

★ The Sensitive Period for Small Objects is the intense focus on small details that stems from the need for classification.

★ The Sensitive Period for Language is the effortless acquiring of language due to the child's intense interest in all forms of human language.

Children pass through other Sensitive Periods for Spatial Relationships, Grace and Courtesy, Refinement of the Senses, Writing, Reading, Music, and Mathematics primarily after age 3.

Understanding your child's Sensitive Periods is one of the keys to understanding what they need in their environment and why they are behaving in a certain way.

THE BASICS OF TODDLER DEVELOPMENT

Toddlers are amazing! They're interested in everything about the adult world and they're also fiercely independent. They've grown so much in such a short time, yet they're in an in-between stage, not a baby anymore, but not quite a preschooler either. They have big emotions and don't always know how to process them, which can lead to meltdowns. But they are also curious, full of discovery and joy, and can love unconditionally and completely!

With so much to explore in the world, toddlers need our help. They need the ability to freely and safely move their bodies. They need to feel like empowered, valued family members by completing daily or practical life skills like washing dishes or helping with the laundry. They need clear and consistent guidelines and limits from their caregivers. Above all else, they need caring adults who allow them to process what's being shown to them. They need someone who helps them communicate and strengthen their language skills and genuinely tries to understand their needs.

This book can help adults provide what toddlers need. The 60 activities are divided into 5 main categories that are the most important areas of a toddler's development:

Motor Skills

This category is all about your toddler moving freely! Toddlers are in a Sensitive Period for Movement because physical activity is essential for building strong cognitive connections and bodies. There are easy-to-play games that strengthen both a child's small and large muscle groups. This helps feed their sensitive period for maximum effort and helps refine their body movements. Chapter 3 focuses on children exploring and mastering important skills safely while having fun!

Art

Creative exploration helps children build self-confidence. Everything from experimenting with color mixing to a toddler's first lines on paper with a crayon is important self-expression in Montessori. Chapter 4 focuses on children expressing themselves creatively and helping them communicate ideas.

Practical Life

Toddlers love to help! They're fiercely independent and want to contribute to their world. Practical life is a cornerstone of Montessori, and the activities in chapter 5 focus on providing your child easy opportunities to help around the house, which aids their self-reliance and confidence.

Sensory Stimulation

The world is a sensorial experience and toddlers love discovering it! Strengthening sensory skills is important in Montessori, as these are the skills that are used later for mathematics and reading. Chapter 6 helps strengthen a child's awareness, allowing them to refine each sense and try new things.

Language

Montessori views language as all the ways humans communicate. Toddlers especially need to feel confident in their ownership over their words and their bodies. Chapter 7 offers opportunities to help your toddler build their vocabulary, phonetic awareness, and social-emotional awareness through fun games.

THE BASICS OF RAISING A TODDLER THE MONTESSORI WAY

Toddlers can be messy, fussy, and downright exhausting! Or, that's the common impression of them. The Montessori Method challenges these ideas about toddler behavior and personality, instead asking adults to look at the young child differently.

Toddlers are strong-willed and curious! From a developmental standpoint, they finally have the ability to communicate and to physically move how they want. The world is theirs to discover.

The Montessori Method looks at toddlers' social-neurological stage of development to understand how to support them in this development. We observe the child and try to understand their motives. Are they climbing onto the counter to reach something? Are they frustrated because they can't verbally communicate their wants? The Montessori Method prepares the environment to give a child freedom within limits. We bring the water glasses and food down to their level, fostering their independence. We use role modeling, giving children language and opportunities to express themselves. Most important, we, as the adults, see each unique child for who they are and encourage their own desire to learn and discover at their own pace.

Terrible Twos

These are often what we are warned about. The meltdowns, the constant questions, the fact that it always has to be their way! It can be exhausting for caregivers, but the Montessori philosophy looks at these behaviors as the result of a toddler's stage of development. This can help shed some light on the most irksome of these behaviors. Toddlers are in the Sensitive Period for Order. They feel most secure when they can predict what is going to happen in their day. This order carries through into every aspect of their day and may be the reason your child has a meltdown over a sandwich cut into triangles instead of rectangles!

Montessori Twos

Montessori families and educators approach these "terrible two" behaviors of big feelings, constant questions, and a need for power in a different way, and the difference in results is very rewarding! A carefully prepared environment that has less choice to get frustrated about offers a toddler the opportunity for control. This can be done with everything from laying out two outfit options for them to choose from to offering two different types of snacks for them to prepare. Having a predictable spot for each activity or toy your child uses and a way for them to easily put it back in the same spot helps limit frustration and builds independence. Finally, changing our language and implementing more grace in our daily lives as adults can help us navigate a toddler's big feelings. This can be as simple as verbally recognizing a child's feelings, such as, "I see you look angry at having to put away your toy. I get angry, too, sometimes." Building connections while sidestepping power struggles with children helps build a resilient and self-confident child.

It follows that the child
can only develop fully by
means of experience on
[their] environment. We call
such experience "work."

—DR. MARIA MONTESSORI

CHAPTER 2

ACTIVITIES THE MONTESSORI WAY

You are now ready for the Montessori activities and how to put it all together! In this chapter, you'll learn what makes a Montessori activity different from traditional young toddler toys and how you can ensure your activities keep with the Montessori Method. You'll learn how to create a prepared environment for your toddler in your home, outside, and even on the go when needed, and how to prepare for the activities. And finally, I'll give you some helpful tips and tricks. These will be little, easy-to-remember ideas to try as you do these activities with your child—extra extensions to encourage your toddler to explore, learn, and most important, have fun.

UNDERSTANDING A MONTESSORI ACTIVITY

Montessori activities (sometimes called "works") are different from traditional children's toys. In this section, I'll help you gain an understanding of why all these aspects are important to child development and how each of them works to empower the child and foster their independence.

Skill Focused

Montessori activities focus on one specific skill at a time. Activities that have a single, self-correcting skill reduce overstimulation in the child. An example of this is the color-sorting activity found in chapter 6. In this activity, the items to be sorted are all exactly the same except for their color. This built-in control of error helps a child independently correct their work without the need for an adult. Other examples of different skills these activities will focus on include gross motor body movements, vocabulary building, and life skill independence.

Complete

One of the reasons Montessori activities are so successful is that they have a clear beginning, middle, and end.

Let's look at a sweeping activity. The beginning is the awareness from the child that there are crumbs on the floor. The beginning could also be the adult inviting the child to an activity. The child goes to the place in their prepared environment where they know they will find the tools they need.

The middle of the activity is the child's purposeful work. This portion of the activity can sometimes last a long time. Don't worry, this is completely normal for toddlers! They may do the middle of the activity over and over.

The end of the activity is when the child is finished. They could be very clearly showing us they are done, by putting their tools away, or the sign could be more subtle, such as the child losing focus. It's okay if this happens. Help the child return their materials to the correct spot to use next time.

Prepared

Montessori activities are carefully prepared before they are shown to a child. They are appealing to the eye and have everything the child needs to complete the activity independently. Having only what your child needs in an activity and ensuring it is carefully prepared to be self-correcting, so your toddler can complete and correct the work independently, helps your child learn independently!

Free within Limits

In Montessori, a child is free to choose their activities within the prepared environment. They choose what activity they're curious about, and they also choose how long to use it. Even if you have an activity in mind to show the child, it is up to them to choose whether or not to agree to work with the material. This can sometimes be frustrating for adults, especially when working with toddlers! However, this is essential to building the child's concentration, independence, and love of learning.

HOW TO PREPARE

Montessori spaces and activities are simple and inviting. Often they take extra time to prepare, but the benefits are worth it! Each activity in this book explains the prep process, so you'll see how long the prep takes, what you'll need, and how the space should be set up before you begin.

How to Prepare an Activity

Let's look at how to prepare Montessori activities quickly and easily. The activities in part 2 have a clear recipe for success. The target skill tells you what developmental area your toddler is strengthening. The materials, prep time, and prep instructions give you a list of the items needed to do each activity and the steps and time it will take to prep the materials for use with your toddler. Sometimes activities will require a container, such as a basket or tray, and I've placed those in the materials list, too, so you will know everything that you need beforehand.

Some of these activities call for small objects like animal figurines, which if too small could be a choking hazard for your child. Be mindful of your child's age and development when choosing what size objects to use and what activities to share with your child!

Next, let's take a look at what a Montessori Prepared Environment is and how you can quickly and easily set one up in your home!

How to Prepare an Activity Space

A beautiful, well-organized Montessori space can draw both you and your child into it. It doesn't have to be big or fancy! It could be a room, a small area, or even just a few baskets on a shelf. It might even be outside. Whatever the size, it just has to work for your family. If it doesn't, you and your child will become frustrated.

There are some simple guidelines for creating this space that make all the difference. Accessibility and safety for the child are the most important. Low shelves, baskets, and hooks help a child independently move in the space. A small mat the child rolls out on a floor helps them see their workspace and keep their materials tidy. You can easily use what you already have at home to help your child's activities become more organized.

Paring down the space to have only a few activities out at a time helps a toddler's Sensitive Period for Order. They know where each material lives and how to put it away. Rotating a few materials at a time into a child's prepared environment keeps things uncluttered and a toddler's interest level high. Book baskets, with a few books at a time, help get kids interested in reading. Making the space beautiful helps attract the child's curiosity. Art placed at their eye level and safe plants help beautify a space. Family photos or printed images of animals are often a toddler's favorite!

GETTING THE MOST OUT OF THIS BOOK

The 60 activities in this book are designed to engage a child from 1 to 3 years old in a variety of fun ways, both indoors and outdoors. It's all about building a connection with your child, trying new things, and having a lot of fun!

Each chapter has about 12 activities organized from easiest to hardest following the Montessori Methodology. Each of the activities comes with a well laid-out, step-by-step sequence of a beginning, middle, and end, starting with inviting your child to a new activity and modeling how to take the tray from their activity shelf to a worktable or mat, your child doing the purposeful work of the activity, and indicating when they are done and modeling how to return the activity back to their shelf. To help keep a child focused, each activity concentrates on one main skill. Note that the parental prep is completed before the beginning of the activity. Some tips that can help you modify the activity to make it more suitable for your child's abilities are at the end of each activity.

BEFORE YOU BEGIN

The following are some helpful Montessori tips and tricks to know before presenting the activities to your child.

Slow Hands, Limit Words

If you're talking, toddlers will focus on your voice instead of what your hands are doing. When showing an activity, limit the amount of talking and slow your body down to help your child clearly follow directions.

Observe First

Your observation is the key to your child strengthening their independence. After you've demonstrated the activity, observe your child and make notes of what worked. Step in only when asked by the child or safety is an issue.

Model Behavior

Toddlers are absorbent sponges! Modeling how to sweep, pour carefully, or put away an activity helps them build their independence. They will one day begin to do it themselves. If a child expresses frustration at a task, gently offer ways to help them complete it.

Verbal Cues

Verbal cues are often hard for toddlers to follow. Help them by adding actions and other body movements to your conversation. Toddlers find these much easier to follow. You can also slow your words or repeat your message. Offering gentle language and patience helps your child do what you're asking.

Freedom

In Montessori learning, it's very important to allow the child to use a material for as long as they like and whatever way they like, as long as it's safe. If your child is enjoying an activity, help them build their concentration by letting them work on it until they show they are finished.

A child who has become master of [their] acts through long and repeated exercises, and who has been encouraged by the pleasant and interesting activities in which [they have] been engaged, is a child filled with health and joy and remarkable for [their] calmness and discipline.

—DR. MARIA MONTESSORI

PART 2

Montessori Activities

These 60 Montessori activities include crafts, matching games, music exploration, and life skills. Each simple activity builds your toddler's independence, self-confidence, and creativity, so let's dive into the fun!

It is high time that
movement came to be
regarded from a new
point of view in
educational theory.

—DR. MARIA MONTESSORI

CHAPTER 3

LET'S MOVE: ACTIVITIES FOR MOTOR SKILLS

Starting gross motor movement activities early can leave a lasting positive impact on your child's coordination, independence, self-confidence, and most important, their physical health. Plus, movement activities are fun and easy to do with toddlers! They bring to a child a love of being active and outside in nature that will last their lifetime!

From the earliest days when your toddler learns to reach for objects, to later when they start to walk, your toddler is building important developmental skills. Montessori nurtures these skills by offering children exciting opportunities to explore their prepared environment safely and by targeting one skill at a time. Targeted skills include throwing, catching, and lifting heavy objects. Examples of these and more are listed in the easy Montessori activities that follow, so let's get started!

1. Maximum Effort: Walker Wagon Push

TARGET SKILL: GROSS MOTOR LEGS
TODDLER AGE: 1
PREP TIME: 1 TO 5 MINUTES

Young toddlers are in their Sensitive Period for Maximum Effort and love to test their physical limits. We can aid this by giving them safe and exciting ways to build their strength. This activity strengthens a child's core muscles and aids their coordination and independent movement.

MATERIALS:

☐ Plastic jug
☐ Small, wheeled cart

ᶾCautionᵋ
Supervision is required.

PREP: Fill a large plastic jug with water and place it in the cart. Clear a space where your toddler can freely move with the cart without running over or tripping on objects.

BEGINNING: Ensure the jug is level. Invite your child to the cart and demonstrate how to push it slowly with two hands safely on the handlebar.

MIDDLE: Now it's their turn! Allow the child a turn pushing it themselves. They may enjoy adding a toy to the cart and giving it a ride, or even try backing up with the cart.

END: Show your child how to return the cart to its prepared spot so they will know where it is in the future for when they want to return to this activity.

Try this! Decrease or increase the amount of water in the jug to find the right amount for your child.

2. Beanbag Toss

TARGET SKILL: GROSS MOTOR ARM CONTROL
TODDLER AGE: 1 TO 3
PREP TIME: 5 MINUTES

Children love throwing! In Montessori, instead of saying no, we help them find appropriate and purposeful ways of doing things safely while having a lot of fun.

MATERIALS:

☐ Beanbags of different weights (or make your own by filling cloth bags with dried beans)
☐ Storage basket with handles
☐ A hoop

> *Caution*
> *Beanbags should be heavy but easily thrown by your child.*

PREP: Place all the beanbags in a basket and lay the hoop down 3 feet away.

BEGINNING: Bring the child to the prepared space and show them the basket of beanbags. Allow them to feel each of the bags and use some describing words, such as, "heavy, heavier, heaviest." Pick up one of the beanbags and show your toddler how to throw it into the hoop.

MIDDLE: Now it's your child's turn! When there are no more bags in the basket, show them how to pick it up and carry it over to the hoop. Help them put the beanbags back in the basket, then start again.

END: When your toddler has finished, model how to put the beanbags back into the basket and return it to the shelf.

Try this! Don't have a hoop? Reuse a box or draw a circle on the ground if you're outside!

3. Moving to Music

TARGET SKILL: CREATIVE BODY EXPRESSION AND BODY AWARENESS
TODDLER AGE: 1 TO 3
PREP TIME: 1 TO 5 MINUTES

Children love listening to music, and this activity will help them build body control and self-confidence.

MATERIALS:

☐ Any device for playing music
☐ Speaker

PREP: Clear an area that's safe for movement and set up a music device and speaker. Choose slow- to medium-paced music to start. Any type is okay as long as it's appropriate for children.

BEGINNING: Invite your toddler to the prepared space and tell them you are going to try something new! Begin playing the music and, without saying anything, move your body to the music. This is all about creative expression, so have fun!

MIDDLE: Observe to see if your child automatically begins moving, too. It should remain fun yet safe. It doesn't matter if they match the beat of the music; what's important is that you are both having fun! You can try slower or faster songs.

END: When your child is finished, turn off the music and use this moment as a communication tool. Ask them if they liked the music. If they did, make an observation note about the type of music it was and how your child responded.

Try this! Self-conscious about dancing? Me too! Try changing the styles of music and dancing slower, faster, or sillier.

4. Montessori Coin Drop

TARGET SKILL: PINCER GRASP
TODDLER AGE: 1 TO 3
PREP TIME: 5 TO 10 MINUTES

Fine motor skills are extremely important in Montessori, and this DIY version of the classic coin box activity is a fun way to support pre-writing skills!

MATERIALS:

- ☐ Canister with soft plastic lid
- ☐ Knife
- ☐ 4 or 5 poker chips
- ☐ Small bowl
- ☐ Tray with handles

PREP: Cut a slit into the soft plastic lid of the canister with the knife. Ensure it is wide enough for a poker chip to easily slide through. Put the poker chips in the bowl and the bowl and canister on the tray. Place the tray on a shelf in the child's prepared space.

BEGINNING: Invite your toddler to the shelf and show them this new activity. Model carrying the tray to a worktable. Remove all the items. Take one of the chips from the bowl by pinching it with your thumb and index finger. Slowly move your hand so the chip is just over the slot in the canister. Drop the chip into the canister. Model it one more time.

MIDDLE: Offer a turn to your child. Observe how easily they can place the chip in the hole. They can do the activity as long as they like!

END: When your child is finished, show them how to return the tray to the shelf.

Use this! Don't have poker chips? Try cutting 2-inch circles out of recycled cardboard.

5. Play Silks and Music

TARGET SKILL: SPATIAL AND BODY AWARENESS
TODDLER AGE: 1 TO 3
PREP TIME: 1 TO 5 MINUTES

Play silks are a beautiful way of connecting music with movement. This activity builds on a toddler's spatial awareness and body control.

MATERIALS:

- ☐ Any device to play music
- ☐ Small storage basket with handles
- ☐ 2 to 4 play silks in different colors

PREP: Gather all the materials and bring them to a safe area for free movement. Place the play silks in the basket so your child can easily choose a color.

BEGINNING: After inviting your toddler to the space, play music and choose a play silk. Ideally the music is soft, slow, and calming for this activity. Ask the child if they would like to choose a play silk. Hold your silk and begin moving it in time with the music creatively.

MIDDLE: Ask your child to join in, too. They may not move exactly as you do, and that's okay! Have fun and experiment creatively with your movements and your toddler may decide to follow your lead.

END: When the music ends or your toddler is finished, model how to put the play silk back in the storage basket. Pick up the basket and show them where it will be kept in their space for future use.

Use this! Don't have play silks? Try a scarf or bandana.

Try this! Try changing the music to explore different body movements.

6. Wheelbarrow Work: Outdoor Fun

TARGET SKILL: GROSS MOTOR DEVELOPMENT
TODDLER AGE: 1 TO 3
PREP TIME: 5 MINUTES

Children love engaging in outdoor purposeful play, and using a wheelbarrow strengthens hand-eye coordination and gross motor development.

MATERIALS:

- ☐ Child-size wheelbarrow
- ☐ Objects of different weights

PREP: Prepare an outdoor space that's clear of hazards and where your toddler can move around freely. Place the wheelbarrow and objects in this space far enough apart so the child has to walk to get them.

BEGINNING: Tell your child you're going to show them a new tool, and introduce it by saying, "This is a wheelbarrow." Tell them, "This is how you use it," and then without speaking, bend, and lift it using your hands, and walk a few steps. Place the wheelbarrow down and ask if your child would like a turn.

MIDDLE: Once your toddler has been walking with the wheelbarrow, show them how to place an object in it and then walk to the next object. Observe how they move with the wheelbarrow and which objects they are choosing to carry in it.

END: When finished, remove the objects from the wheelbarrow. Show the child where it will be stored and tell them it will be there for the next time.

Use this! A small cart works well, too, if you don't have a child-size wheelbarrow.

7. Bowling Games

TARGET SKILL: GROSS MOTOR SKILLS
TODDLER AGE: 1 TO 3
PREP TIME: 1 TO 5 MINUTES

Toddlers love cause and effect, and this game encourages this tendency while building core strength and balance.

MATERIALS:

- ☐ Wooden or rubber ball
- ☐ Small wooden bowling pins
- ☐ Small storage basket with handles

›Caution‹
This game is meant for rolling the ball. If throwing happens, direct your child to another activity like Beanbag Toss (page 21).

PREP: Organize the ball and pins in the basket and place it in the child's prepared space.

BEGINNING: Invite your toddler to the prepared space and tell them you are going to play a game! Model carrying the basket to an open space and setting up the pins. Tell the child you are ready to begin the game. Roll the ball toward the pins and observe how many get knocked down.

MIDDLE: Offer a turn to your child. Even if no pins fall over when they roll the ball, simply ask them to try again. They may get creative and that's okay! As long as their movements are safe, observe how they are knocking down the pins.

END: When they are finished, show them how to pick up the ball and pins and put them back in the basket. Then show them where this activity will be stored in their prepared space.

Use this! Don't have bowling pins? Toilet paper tubes or plastic cups work great, too!

8. Ball Games

TARGET SKILL: GROSS MOTOR SKILLS
TODDLER AGE: 1 TO 3
PREP TIME: 1 TO 5 MINUTES

A ball is one of the simplest and best materials for building gross motor skills!

MATERIALS:

☐ Large rubber ball

PREP: Prepare a storage space where the ball will be kept. Bring the ball to the area where you will do the activity with your toddler.

BEGINNING: Sitting on the floor close to your toddler, show them the ball. If they are very young, introduce it by saying, "This is a ball." With your feet and legs apart, roll the ball gently to your child. Have them roll it back to you.

MIDDLE: When your child is ready for a more challenging game, you can stand up and try a number of different games, such as kicking the ball (around 2 years old) or standing and bouncing the ball with both hands. Experiment with different ways to use the ball each time. Some toddlers will love just kicking it and chasing after it!

END: Each time your game is finished, let your toddler know where the ball will be stored and model putting it away until they can do it independently.

Try this! There are endless games that a toddler with a ball can try. If you don't have the space for a large rubber ball, try using a smaller one instead. Use different balls, if possible, for rolling games, throwing games, and kicking games.

9. Up, Up, Up: Climbing Fun

TARGET SKILL: STRENGTHEN CORE AND LEG MUSCLES
TODDLER AGE: 1 TO 3
PREP TIME: 1 TO 5 MINUTES

Toddlers love climbing and seem to climb everywhere! We can help them build this key developmental skill safely and purposefully.

MATERIALS:

☐ Wooden climbing triangle or stairs

◦Caution◦
Toddlers are fast! This activity needs your full attention.

PREP: If using a wooden climbing triangle, set it up in your space. Bare feet are best for this activity and a soft, carpeted area underneath is ideal.

BEGINNING: Invite your toddler over to the material to remove their socks and shoes. At the stairs, model for them how to walk carefully. At the wooden triangle, show them where to place their hands. If it's a young child, guide their hands to a bar they can hold and then show them how to put one foot on the lowest bar.

MIDDLE: Allow your toddler to explore their own movements. They may want to go up and down again and again, and that's part of the fun! This builds their self-confidence and motivation. You may find your toddler masters going up first, but needs more help with getting down.

END: If the triangle will be packed away, you can do this now and tell your child it will be ready for next time.

Try this! Outside stairs are some of the best! Give your toddler the opportunity to go up and down a variety of different types of stairways and ramps outside to build more core muscles and concentration.

10. Hop, Skip, and Jump

TARGET SKILL: GROSS MOTOR LOWER BODY SKILLS
TODDLER AGE: 1 TO 3
PREP TIME: 1 TO 5 MINUTES

These movements make up so many of the games played by older children, and they are so important in toddler development!

MATERIALS:

☐ Sidewalk chalk

PREP: Draw lines on the pavement with chalk. They can be straight or wavy!

BEGINNING: Invite your child to stand near one of the lines and tell them you are going to do a movement game. Standing beside them and behind the line, demonstrate hopping over the line with two feet. Allow them to try next. It's okay if their movements aren't the same as yours!

MIDDLE: Continue trying different hops, skips, and jumps over and along some of the lines you've drawn. It's all about having fun, so don't be afraid to get silly! Let your child lead some movements around the lines and observe how they choose to move.

END: When finished, let your toddler know that you can do this again another day. If you are in an area where you can clean off the lines with a hose and water, your toddler may love to help!

Try this! Can't get outside today? You can easily adapt some of the movements of this game to indoors. Try jumping from pillow to pillow or between couch cushions placed on the floor.

11. Walking on the Line

TARGET SKILL: BODY AWARENESS AND CONTROL
TODDLER AGE: 2 TO 3
PREP TIME: 5 MINUTES

This is the classic Montessori game for building balance and refining body movement—and toddlers love trying it!

MATERIALS:

☐ Wide roll of painter's tape
☐ 2 or 3 small objects

PREP: Clear a spot to make a straight line or an ellipse on the floor or ground with the tape.

BEGINNING: Invite the child to the line and to remove their shoes and socks. Show them how to slowly and carefully walk on the line to the end of the tape or around the ellipse.

MIDDLE: The child can try walking back and forth on the line as many times as they like! They may want to hold a small object and try to walk carefully without dropping it. Although the end goal is for them to walk with one foot in front of the other as they get older, it's okay for them to walk in any way they like now as long as it's a controlled movement.

END: When the child shows they are finished, they can put their socks and shoes back on. They can help pull the tape from the floor if they are interested.

Try this! Try changing your movements on the line with older children. They can walk on tiptoe, hold objects in their hands, or even balance a small ball on a spoon.

12. Toddler Animal Yoga

TARGET SKILL: CONTROL OF BODY MOVEMENTS
TODDLER AGE: 2 TO 3
PREP TIME: 1 TO 5 MINUTES

Yoga is such a great way for toddlers to slow down and build body awareness.

MATERIALS:

☐ Soft carpet or yoga mat

PREP: If you're using a yoga mat, roll it out in the prepared space. Dress in comfortable clothing you and your toddler can easily move in.

BEGINNING: Invite your child to the prepared space and tell them you are both going to do some animal poses! Start by standing comfortably on your mat or carpet. Reach up with your arms over your head and say, "We can reach like a giraffe." Stretch up and pretend your hand is a giraffe eating leaves from tall branches.

MIDDLE: Try different animal poses with your child. Have fun and don't be shy! Curl up like a cat, bend down and use your arm like an elephant's trunk, or sit cross-legged and move your knees up and down to "flap like a butterfly." It's okay if your child doesn't do the poses exactly or tries different things on their own.

END: When finished, show the child how to roll the yoga mat and place it in a space where they can easily find it for next time.

Try this! Need a little inspiration? There are lots of fabulous kids' yoga videos, music, and apps out there. Try one out and enjoy!

Imagination does not
become great until
human beings, given the
courage and the strength,
use it to create.

—DR. MARIA MONTESSORI

CHAPTER 4

ART IS FOR ALL

Art is one of the most important ways a child shows their inner self-expression! In Montessori, the introduction of different sensorial experiences while the child is still in their absorbent mind stage of development is of the utmost importance, and art is a great way to achieve this. We offer the child open-ended, process-based activities instead of the ready-made typical crafts that focus on the end product. We allow a child to experiment with different art mediums, such as paint, wax crayons, and even fiber arts. This helps a young child strengthen their independence by allowing them to experiment and make choices.

The following art activities invite your toddler to explore their own creative expression through sensory experiences. From the simplest finger squishing play dough to experimenting with color mixing to creating with beading, your child will begin to build their self-expression and sense of self.

13. Montessori Glue Tray

TARGET SKILL: HAND-EYE COORDINATION
TODDLER AGE: 1 TO 3
PREP TIME: 5 TO 10 MINUTES

In Montessori, we help toddlers learn to glue in an easy and organized way.

MATERIALS:

- ☐ Paper scraps, ribbon scraps, and various items to glue
- ☐ Small container
- ☐ Container with screw-on lid
- ☐ White craft glue
- ☐ Wooden tray with handles
- ☐ Wipeable mat
- ☐ Small sheets of paper
- ☐ Short paintbrush

⟩Caution⟨
Supervision
is recommended.

PREP: Choose 3 to 5 scrap items and place them in the container. Fill the second container with a small amount of glue and screw the lid on. Put all the materials on the tray and place it on a shelf.

BEGINNING: Invite your child to come and try some new artwork. Model how to bring the tray to the worktable. Lay the mat on the table and arrange the glue, paper, container of scraps, and the paintbrush on the mat. Model dipping the brush in glue and brushing it on the paper. Then choose a loose item to stick to it.

MIDDLE: Now it's your toddler's turn! Observe and offer help if needed. They can choose something from the container to glue on. It might get messy, but keep going—that's part of the fun!

END: When your child is finished, help them put all the items except their new artwork back on the tray. Model how to return the tray to the shelf.

Try this! A wet cloth close by will help minimize sticky fingers!

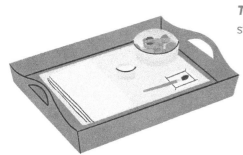

14. Hole Punching

TARGET SKILL: HAND STRENGTH
TODDLER AGE: 1 TO 3
PREP TIME: 1 TO 5 MINUTES

Hole punching is a favorite in Montessori classrooms, as it builds so much concentration and hand strength. Toddlers at home love it, too!

MATERIALS:

- Small strips of paper
- Small container
- Craft hole punch
- Wooden tray with handles

PREP: Place the strips of paper in the container and gather all the materials on the tray.. Place it on a shelf.

BEGINNING: Invite a child to the shelf and tell them you have something to show them. Model how to bring the tray to a table and place all the items on the table. Choose a strip of paper from the container and tell the child you are going to make a special design in the paper. Punch the paper with the hole punch and show your toddler the result. Now it's their turn!

MIDDLE: Help your child only if they ask or are showing signs of frustration. They can continue until there is no room left on the paper. Show them how to choose a new strip and start again.

END: When finished, model how to return everything to the tray and place the tray on the shelf.

Try this! Sometimes larger hole punches are easier to push down. Try different shapes to get a variety of cutouts. Older toddlers may want to glue these with the gluing tray.

15. Rainbow Hand Painting

TARGET SKILL: SENSORIAL COLOR EXPLORATION
TODDLER AGE: 1 TO 3
PREP TIME: 1 TO 5 MINUTES

Strengthening sensorial input while experimenting with color mixing is a great combination for toddlers.

MATERIALS:

☐ Washable tempera paints
☐ Paper plate
☐ White paper
☐ Paintbrush
☐ Smock or Montessori apron
☐ Plastic tray

⟩Caution⟨
Supervision is recommended.

PREP: Gather all the materials on the tray and place it on the shelf.

BEGINNING: Show the materials you've gathered to your toddler and tell them you're going to try something. Model carrying the tray to the child's worktable. Arrange all the materials on the table and tell your toddler that for this activity they will need to wear an apron. Pour a small amount of each paint color onto the paper plate.

MIDDLE: Show your child how to dip the brush in the red paint and paint a horizontal line across the inside of your hand near your fingertips. Continue with the next color you choose, painting under the first line. When your hand is covered, press your hand onto the paper and see the results! Your child may want to jump into the fun before you've modeled the entire lesson, and that's great! Let them explore!

END: When finished, model how to clean up and put everything back in the basket or tray. Then return it to the shelf.

Try this! Experiment and have fun; your child may prefer to just finger paint!

16. Sidewalk Chalk Design and Erase

TARGET SKILL: CREATIVE EXPRESSION
TODDLER AGE: 1 TO 3
PREP TIME: 1 TO 3 MINUTES

Montessori loves incorporating the outdoors into learning. Expanding a child's physical area not only helps build spatial awareness, but also promotes gross motor movement with creativity!

MATERIALS:

☐ Small bucket of water
☐ Sidewalk chalk
☐ Large, flat paintbrush

PREP: Prepare an outdoor asphalt or cement area by removing any obstacles. Fill the bucket with water.

BEGINNING: Bring your prepared materials outside and show them to your toddler, naming each one to build vocabulary. Take chalk and draw a straight line with it slowly so your toddler can observe your hand movements. Draw another line of your choice. You don't have to be the best artist; your toddler will love it! Now tell your toddler that you are going to use the water to wash away the line. Slowly dip the brush into the water and trace over your first line.

MIDDLE: It's your toddler's turn! Observe first before interrupting if possible, because creativity is key here. They may choose to trace your chalk lines, make their own, or use the water and paintbrush for something else, and that's okay, too. This is also a great time to experiment with language!

END: When finished, model how to carefully dump the remaining water and clean up.

Try this! Take this activity on the go to the park!

17. Animal Rubber Stamps

TARGET SKILL: SELF-EXPRESSION
TODDLER AGE: 1 TO 3
PREP TIME: 1 TO 5 MINUTES

Toddlers love the cause and effect of rubber stamping and the process of stamping the ink pad to get a result.

MATERIALS:

- ☐ 2 or 3 rubber stamps with animal designs
- ☐ Ink pad
- ☐ 3 or 4 small squares of paper
- ☐ Wooden tray with handles

PREP: Gather all the materials on the tray and place it on the shelf.

BEGINNING: Show your toddler the tray and tell them you have a new artwork to show them. Model bringing the tray to a worktable or mat. Remove everything from the tray while naming each item for your toddler. Show them how to place one of the stamps on the ink pad and gently push down. Tell them something special is going to happen, then slowly and gently stamp the paper.

MIDDLE: It's your toddler's turn to try! They can choose a stamp and use their creative expression to experiment with different techniques. They may want to stamp one stamp over and over, and that's great!

END: When finished, model how to return all the materials to the tray, ensure the table is clean, and place the tray on the shelf.

Try this! Stamped paper makes great gift wrap! Try larger sheets of newsprint and different types of stamps.

18. Nature Suncatchers

TARGET SKILL: CREATIVE EXPRESSION
TODDLER AGE: 1 TO 3
PREP TIME: 5 TO 10 MINUTES

Gathered treasures from nature connect a child to the world and bring out their sense of awe and wonder. These suncatchers are a lovely keepsake!

MATERIALS:

- ☐ Contact paper, cut into large circles (2 per suncatcher)
- ☐ Found nature objects like flowers, leaves, and small twigs
- ☐ Hole punch
- ☐ Yarn or string
- ☐ Wooden tray with handles

PREP: Gather all the materials on the tray and place it on your toddler's shelf.

BEGINNING: Invite your toddler to the shelf and tell them you have a new artwork to show them! Model bringing the tray to a worktable. Peel the backing off one contact paper circle and place it on the table, sticky-side up.

MIDDLE: It's time for your toddler to try! Allow them to choose items to place on the contact paper. Repeat this until the paper is filled or your toddler is finished.

END: When finished, peel the backing off the second circle. Help your toddler guide it to match the first circle, pressing down gently. Your treasures are now sealed! Hole punch the top and thread yarn through. Hang the suncatcher in the window! Show your toddler how to clean up, return unused materials to the tray, and put the tray back on the shelf.

Try this! Nature treasures can be found at the park, on your street, or can even be a fresh flower from the store!

19. Play Dough Fun

TARGET SKILL: HAND STRENGTH
TODDLER AGE: 1½ TO 3
PREP TIME: 5 TO 10 MINUTES

Play dough builds hand strength and also gives a toddler an amazing sensory experience.

MATERIALS:

- ☐ Small washable mat
- ☐ Wooden tray with handles
- ☐ Store-bought or homemade play dough
- ☐ Child-size table and chair

Caution
Toddlers love putting things in their mouths. Make sure your play dough is safe to eat.

PREP: Place the mat on the tray, put a fist-size amount of play dough on the tray, and place it on a shelf in your child's space.

BEGINNING: Invite your child to the shelf and show them the tray containing the play dough. Tell them you'd like to show them something new. Model how to carry the tray to the table and chair. Tell your child about the play dough using descriptive words to build their vocabulary. This is the fun part! Begin molding the dough in your hands and then offer a turn to your child.

MIDDLE: Continue using the play dough in any way your toddler likes! This is a sensory and creative experience for your child, so they might just squish the dough, and that's okay!

END: When your toddler is finished, show them how to roll the mat and place it on the tray, then return the tray to the shelf.

Try this! Add spices and essential oils to your dough for a different sensorial experience!

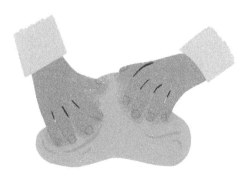

20. Sticker Fun

TARGET SKILL: CONCENTRATION AND FINE MOTOR SKILLS
TODDLER AGE: 1½ TO 3
PREP TIME: 5 TO 10 MINUTES

Children love stickers, and they are amazing for improving hand strength and concentration.

MATERIALS:

- ☐ Stickers of various sizes
- ☐ Small container for stickers
- ☐ Precut pieces of paper that fit on the tray
- ☐ Wooden tray with handles

⟩Caution⟨
Toddlers are fast! Most paper is non-toxic, but this still requires supervision.

PREP: Gather all the materials on the tray and place it on the shelf.

BEGINNING: With the child, model taking the tray off the shelf and bringing it to a worktable or mat. Show your toddler how to remove the materials from the tray. Show them how to peel off the backing from the sticker and place the sticker on the paper. Then it's your child's turn!

MIDDLE: Creativity is the object here, as is patience! It might take your child a long time to pull the backing off the sticker, but that's okay. They are working hard at being independent.

END: When your toddler is finished, help them return all the items except their artwork back to the tray and return the tray to the shelf. Model how to clean up.

Try this! Help your child be independent by using larger stickers or starting to peel a corner of the backing and letting them finish independently.

21. Introducing Scissors the Montessori Way

TARGET SKILL: HAND-EYE COORDINATION
TODDLER AGE: 1½ TO 3
PREP TIME: 1 TO 5 MINUTES

Montessori introduces scissor skills safely and in a fun way that builds fine motor skills!

MATERIALS:

- ☐ Child-size safety scissors
- ☐ Thin rectangles of paper, about ½ inch by 4 inches
- ☐ Small container
- ☐ Wooden tray with handles

⟩Caution⟨
Supervision required.

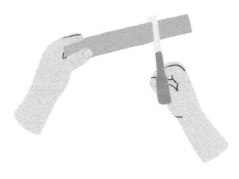

PREP: Gather all the materials on the tray and place it on a shelf.

BEGINNING: Show your toddler the tray and model bringing it to a worktable. Name everything on the tray and model how to carefully pick up the scissors. Tell your toddler that we make scissors move by opening and closing our hands. Hold a strip of paper in your opposite hand and slowly cut through the strip, allowing your child to see each step. When the strip is cut, it's their turn! Help them place their fingers in the scissor holes and practice opening and closing their hand. Tell them to take a strip and open their scissor hand. Place the strip between the open scissors. Your toddler can then cut through it.

MIDDLE: Toddlers love repetition. Patience is key! Offer help if needed. If their snips aren't perfect, it's part of the learning fun.

END: When finished, model how to put the scraps of cut paper in the container and everything back on the tray. Return it to the shelf.

Try this! To increase the difficulty of this activity, try drawing different lines on the paper for your child to follow and cut!

22. Threading Beads

TARGET SKILL: FINE MOTOR DEVELOPMENT
TODDLER AGE: 1½ TO 3
PREP TIME: 1 TO 5 MINUTES

Threading beads helps a toddler develop their fine motor skills, concentration, patterning, and creativity!

MATERIALS:

- ☐ Large wooden beads
- ☐ Shoelace with a wooden skewer stick taped to one end and a knot in the other end
- ☐ Wooden tray with handles

›Caution‹
For a child who still mouths items, supervision is required.

PREP: Gather all the materials on the tray and place it on the shelf.

BEGINNING: Show the child the prepared tray and tell them you have something new to show them. Model bringing the tray to a worktable or mat. Remove all the items from the tray, naming each one. Pick up a bead and show them how to slowly thread the skewer and shoelace through the bead and pull it through. Now it's your toddler's turn!

MIDDLE: This activity requires concentration, but your toddler can do it! Allow them the independence of trying to thread the bead themselves before offering help. They can work as long as they like.

END: When finished, show your child how to place all the materials back on the tray and return it to the shelf.

Try this! When this is too easy, try using thread and smaller beads or pasta.

23. Color Mixing

TARGET SKILL: COLOR THEORY
TODDLER AGE: 2 TO 3
PREP TIME: 5 TO 10 MINUTES

Exploring color theory builds a child's creativity and self-expression.

MATERIALS:

- Food coloring in red, blue, and yellow
- 3 round containers with lids
- Eyedropper
- Sectioned dish or small glass bowls
- Small wooden stick
- Child-size cloth
- Plastic tray

PREP: Put 5 drops of a single food coloring color into each container. Fill each container halfway with water and screw on the lids. Arrange all the materials on a plastic tray.

BEGINNING: Invite your child to come try a new artwork with you. Model carefully bringing the tray to their worktable and arranging the items. Unscrew the lids of the containers, naming each color. Show the child the eyedropper and dip its end into the red water. Demonstrate how to squeeze and draw the liquid into the dropper. Expel the water into one of the sections in your dish or bowl. Now it's your toddler's turn!

MIDDLE: Let them suck up yellow and carefully drop it into the dish or bowl with red. Stir the colors with the stick and see what happens. Continue mixing all the colors they choose—remember, there's no wrong answer!

END: When finished, model how to return the lids to the containers and clean spills with the small cloth. Return all the materials back to the tray and place it on the shelf.

Try this! Try using the color mixes on different papers, such as coffee filters.

24. Toddler Collage Crafts

TARGET SKILL: CREATIVE SELF-EXPRESSION
TODDLER AGE: 2½ TO 3
PREP TIME: 5 TO 10 MINUTES

Once your child has practiced with some of the art activities in this book, it's time to put them together to create and explore.

MATERIALS:

- ☐ Paper scraps, ribbon scraps, photo cutouts, or craft supplies to glue
- ☐ Small container
- ☐ Scissors
- ☐ Container with screw-on lid
- ☐ White craft glue
- ☐ Short paintbrush
- ☐ Small squares of paper
- ☐ Child-size cloth
- ☐ Plastic tray with handles

》Caution 《
*Supervision
is recommended.*

PREP: Gather items to glue in the collage and place them in the small container. Put all the materials on the tray and place it on your child's shelf.

BEGINNING: Show your child the tray and tell them you have a new activity for them. Model carrying the tray to a worktable and removing all the items. Name each of the items once they are laid out on the table and tell your child they can use any of them to make a picture.

MIDDLE: Observe and offer help when needed. Your child may want to lead the way! This is all about the process, and it may get messy, but that's part of the fun!

END: When finished, help your child clean the work area and return the materials on the tray to the shelf.

Try this! Magazine cutouts and stickers work well for collages, too!

Any child who is self-sufficient,
who can tie [their] shoes,
dress or undress [themselves],
reflects in [their] joy and sense
of achievement the image of
human dignity, which is derived
from a sense of independence.

—DR. MARIA MONTESSORI

CHAPTER 5

A DAY IN THE LIFE: ACTIVITIES FOR PRACTICAL LIFE

Practical life is the foundation of the entire Montessori Method! Giving a child the developmental skills needed to strengthen their independence early allows the child to be self-sufficient and confident from a young age. In many of these activities, the preliminary skills needed for later academic success are also practiced.

A prepared environment with well thought-out activities that incorporate practical life helps make everyday acts engaging and fun for toddlers. What we see as boring, they see as new and exciting! Everything from food prep, to caring for plants, to window polishing can be intriguing when done with real, working, child-size tools and prepared in a fun and easy-to-use way. The following activities are quick and easy to set up and provide your child meaningful ways to help contribute to their family rhythm. I can't wait for us to get started!

25. Montessori Jacket Flip

TARGET SKILL: INDEPENDENCE
TODDLER AGE: 1 TO 3
PREP TIME: 1 MINUTE

Helping a toddler master each step of dressing, by isolating certain skills at a time, builds their self-reliance. This Montessori jacket flip can be done by even the youngest toddler with practice.

MATERIALS:

☐ Your toddler's jacket
☐ Small hook

PREP: Hang a hook in your child's dressing space at their height for their jacket to hang on.

BEGINNING: Invite your child to where you have prepared their hook and jacket. Tell them you're going to show them how to put it on by themselves! Take the jacket off the hook and lay it on the floor, front-side up.

MIDDLE: With the jacket laying wide open, walk with your toddler to the top/collar side and stand over the jacket. It should look upside down to you. Model bending down and slipping your arms into the sleeves. Don't worry, it's supposed to look like it's backward! Help your toddler put their arms into the sleeves. When the arms are in, get your toddler to stand up and raise their arms up over their head with the jacket. The jacket will fall behind them onto their back!

END: They can stand up now with their jacket on. It'll get faster as they practice.

Try this! Having a prepared child-size dressing area with a chair and hooks helps little ones get dressed quickly!

26. Open and Close Containers

TARGET SKILL: FINE MOTOR SKILLS
TODDLER AGE: 1 TO 3
PREP TIME: 5 TO 10 MINUTES

The twisting, turning, snapping, and opening to find the treasure inside makes this activity a favorite! It's excellent for building fine motor skills and concentration.

MATERIALS:

☐ Variety of small containers with zippers, clasps, hook and loop fasteners, or twist lids
☐ Play silks or small figurines
☐ Wooden tray with handles

PREP: Place a small play silk or figurine in each container and close it. Gather all the containers onto the tray and place it on a shelf.

BEGINNING: Show your child the activity and invite them to bring it to a worktable or mat. Model how to take each container off the tray. Pick up the easiest-to-open container and slowly model how to open it. Use as few words as possible, like just "open" or "close," so your toddler can concentrate on your hands. Reveal the treasure inside!

MIDDLE: It's your toddler's turn! They can explore opening each container to find the item. Toddlers love repetition, so they may want to do it again and again. Use your Montessori observation and offer help only when necessary. They may want to open everything and dump out the items and that's okay!

END: When finished, replace all the items on the tray and model how to return it to the shelf.

Try this! Clear containers that show the treasures help entice a very young toddler.

27. Helping with the Dishes

TARGET SKILL: INDEPENDENCE
TODDLER AGE: 1 TO 3
PREP TIME: 5 TO 10 MINUTES

Activities rooted in the kitchen are the foundation of practical life. Letting your toddler help wash dishes is a great way to involve them in kitchen life, strengthening their independence.

MATERIALS:

- ☐ Montessori child's kitchen or plastic dish tub
- ☐ Soap dispenser
- ☐ Towel or drying rack
- ☐ Some of your child's dishes
- ☐ Child-size cloth or dish scrubber
- ☐ Smock or Montessori apron

PREP: Fill the sink of the child's kitchen or the dish tub with tepid water. Place the soap dispenser and towel or drying rack close by.

BEGINNING: Show your toddler the prepared activity and invite them to help. Model putting a small amount of soap in the water and creating bubbles with your hand. Place one of your toddler's dishes in the water and model how to clean it with the cloth or scrubber. Use as much vocabulary as you can when describing the activity. Remove the dish and place it in the drying rack or on the towel.

MIDDLE: Show your child how to put on the smock or apron. Invite them to wash a dish. Observe their actions. They may only play in the soapy water and that's okay!

END: When finished, help them clean up any spills, remove the apron, and hang it up.

Try this! Your child can bring dishes to the sink and put them away when finished.

28. Cutting a Banana

TARGET SKILL: INDEPENDENCE
TODDLER AGE: 1 TO 3
PREP TIME: 1 TO 3 MINUTES

Involving a child in the family's meal prep not only helps strengthen family bonding, an important part of Montessori Peace Education, it builds important independence skills, too!

MATERIALS:

☐ Banana
☐ Butter knife
☐ Small cutting board
☐ Fork
☐ Small plate
☐ Child-size cloth

⟩Caution⟨
Toddlers move quickly. Keep your focus on your child.

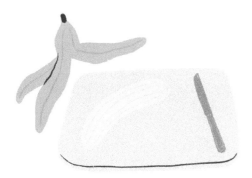

PREP: Prepare the banana by peeling it and laying it horizontally on the cutting board.

BEGINNING: Invite your child to come and see the prepared food area you've created. Show your child the food they will be preparing. Tell them the name of the food they are preparing or, if this is a familiar food, talk about how you are going to prepare it.

MIDDLE: Demonstrate how to hold the knife by placing your hand on the handle and the edge over the banana. Press down on the knife to slice the banana. Offer the knife to your child and ensure they are holding it correctly. Observe your child as they cut through the banana. Use the fork to demonstrate how to pierce the banana and transfer it to a plate.

END: Demonstrate how to clean the work area with the cloth and allow the child to do it, too.

Try this! Once your child has mastered this, experiment with different textured foods and utensils.

29. Plant Care

TARGET SKILL: INDEPENDENCE
TODDLER AGE: 1 TO 3
PREP TIME: 1 TO 5 MINUTES

Caring for living things is an important part of the Montessori Method because it fosters social-emotional awareness. It also builds daily rhythms and routines.

MATERIALS:

- ☐ Small, nontoxic plant in a container
- ☐ Cotton swab
- ☐ Child-size watering can
- ☐ Child-size cloth
- ☐ Small basket

PREP: Place the plant in the child's area where it will live. Gather all the materials into the basket and place it on your toddler's shelf.

BEGINNING: Invite your child to view the basket. In Montessori, we carry the supplies to each plant. Tell your child that these materials are to help care for the plant and name each item. Remove the cotton swab and model how to delicately wipe the leaves. Next, model how to fill the watering can and pour a small amount into the soil.

MIDDLE: Your toddler may want to help at this point. Help their hands if they are unsteady with the cotton swab or the watering can. They may want to water more than the plant needs. Ensure you only have a small amount of water in the can to help them be independent.

END: When finished, help your child wipe any spills with the cloth. Model how to return the materials back in the basket and place it on the shelf for next time!

Try this! Toddlers love to water plants outside, too!

30. Helping with the Laundry

TARGET SKILL: SELF-RELIANCE
TODDLER AGE: 1 TO 3
PREP TIME: 5 TO 10 MINUTES

Doing laundry is a Montessori favorite for toddlers! The multiple steps and gross motor skills help build self-reliance and independence in even the youngest child.

MATERIALS:

- ☐ Child-size drying rack
- ☐ Wooden clothespins
- ☐ Small clothing items (socks work well)
- ☐ Small basket

PREP: Place the drying rack and clothespins in your toddler's prepared environment. Place the clothing items in the basket and put it near the shelf. We'll use dry items for this activity.

BEGINNING: Show your toddler the drying rack and name it. Show your toddler the basket of clothes and take one piece out. Place it on the line and show your toddler how to use a clothespin to attach it. Ask them if they would like to try.

MIDDLE: Your toddler can choose a clothing item and place it on the rack. Observe and help them place the clothespin if necessary. They can also choose to take clothespins off if they'd like! Model how to continue to place clothes on the rack until the basket is empty.

END: When your toddler is finished, remove all the clothes off the rack and place them back in the basket. Invite your child to return the basket to the shelf.

Try this! Invite your toddler to help with the household laundry, too! As they show they have mastered the basics, give them new steps to try.

31. Baby Doll Bath

TARGET SKILL: EMOTIONAL AWARENESS
TODDLER AGE: 1 TO 3
PREP TIME: 1 TO 5 MINUTES

Building emotional and empathetic awareness is fundamental in Montessori. This activity helps children practice these real-life skills.

MATERIALS:

- ☐ Large basin
- ☐ Realistic washable baby doll
- ☐ Child-size cloth
- ☐ Soap
- ☐ Towel

PREP: Gather all the items into the basin and place it in the prepared environment.

BEGINNING: Invite your toddler to come and see the activity. Tell them you are going to give the doll a bath. Fill the basin with tepid water. Gently place the doll into the basin, describing what you are doing. Put some soap and water on the cloth and model how to gently wash the doll. Now it's your toddler's turn to try!

MIDDLE: This is a great opportunity to model nurturing language! Sing as you're washing, or model how to speak lovingly to the doll. You can name each body part, because toddlers love naming games! Remove the doll from the water and show your toddler how to dry it gently with the towel. Your toddler may want to start again at this stage. That's okay! They can work as long as they'd like.

END: When finished, clean up any spills and dump out the water. Replace all the items in the basin and return it to the shelf.

Try this! If your child has younger siblings or family members, invite them to help in the real-life care!

32. Lock Box Fun

TARGET SKILL: SELF-RELIANCE
TODDLER AGE: 1½ TO 3
PREP TIME: 1 TO 5 MINUTES

Lock boxes are perfect for the Montessori Sensitive Period for Small Objects! Curious toddlers love exploring their world and this box helps them refine their fine motor skills, furthering their independence.

MATERIALS:

☐ Montessori lock box

PREP: Place the lock box on the child's shelf.

BEGINNING: Bring your child to the shelf and tell them you have something new! Name the lock box and draw their attention to all the different locks, using as much vocabulary as possible, such as, "This is a slide lock," or "This lock twists open." Invite them to follow you to a worktable and model how to carry the lock box carefully. Place the box on the table and show your child how to open the easiest lock or latch.

MIDDLE: Now it's your toddler's turn! Allow them to explore the box however they want as long as it's safe. Observe and offer help only if necessary. This Montessori activity is all about a child's curiosity and finger strength! Your toddler is developing so much concentration here.

END: When finished, model how to close up each of the latches. Invite your child to carry the lock box back to their shelf.

Try this! You can make a DIY lock box with a small piece of plywood and different latches and locks from the hardware store.

33. Sweeping with Broom and Dustpan

TARGET SKILL: INDEPENDENCE
TODDLER AGE: 1½ TO 3
PREP TIME: 5 TO 10 MINUTES

Sweeping is a popular Montessori practical life activity, because it easily includes your toddler in daily family life while also strengthening hand-eye coordination.

MATERIALS:

- ☐ Painter's tape
- ☐ Pom-poms
- ☐ Container
- ☐ Child-size dustpan and small broom
- ☐ Wooden tray

PREP: Use the painter's tape to mark a 1-foot square on the floor. Put the pom-poms in the container, place the container and remaining materials on the tray, and put the tray in the prepared space.

BEGINNING: Draw your child's attention to the square you've made and tell them you have something special to show them. Bring the tray of materials to the square and set it down nearby. Tell your toddler you're going to do some sweeping, then pour the pom-poms from the container onto the floor. Take the broom and show your toddler how to sweep the pom-poms slowly into the square. Once they're in the square, sweep the pom-poms into the dustpan and dump them back into the container.

MIDDLE: It's all about exploration and repetition! Your toddler may use their hands at the beginning to pick things up. That's okay! Keep observing and guide their hand only when needed.

END: When your toddler is finished, show them how to return everything to the tray and then to the shelf.

Try this! Try the activity without the square for older toddlers who've had some practice!

34. Juicing an Orange

Juicing an orange is a fun food-prep activity where toddlers can see cause and effect. This activity builds their hand strength and concentration.

MATERIALS:

- ☐ 1 orange, cut in half
- ☐ Bowl
- ☐ Citrus juicer
- ☐ Child's glass
- ☐ Child-size cloth
- ☐ Plastic tray with handles

PREP: Gather all the materials on the tray and put it on the child's worktable.

BEGINNING: Bring your child to the prepared activity. Tell them you have something new to show them. Model how to turn the orange upside down over the juicer and bowl, place it on the juicer, and press down and turn so the juice comes out. Ask your toddler if they'd like to try.

MIDDLE: Observe and help your toddler push the orange down while turning it. It can be tricky for young toddlers, but stick with it. You can talk about how the juice is coming out. When both halves of the orange are juiced, place them back on the tray, and pour the juice into the drinking glass.

END: Help your toddler clean up with the cloth and return the materials to the tray. Clean the materials on the tray and prepare it for another day.

Try this! Try using sensorial vocabulary with your child, such as *sour, sweet, juicy,* or *rough,* to describe the orange.

35. Whisking Bubbles

TARGET SKILL: HAND STRENGTH
TODDLER AGE: 2 TO 3
PREP TIME: 5 MINUTES

Whisking bubbles is a delight for a toddler's curiosity and helps build hand strength, too!

MATERIALS:

- ☐ Plastic mixing bowl
- ☐ Small soap dispenser
- ☐ Child-size whisk
- ☐ Child-size cloth
- ☐ Plastic tray

PREP: Gather all the materials onto the tray and prepare in the kitchen at your child's height. Fill the mixing bowl with tepid water.

BEGINNING: Invite your toddler to try something new and show them the prepared tray. Model how to take the materials off the tray. Put a few drops of liquid soap into the water. Model holding the whisk with one hand and the bowl with the other. Begin by moving your whisk in a circular motion.

MIDDLE: Let your toddler try! They may need help to hold the bowl while they whisk. Bubbles will start to form. It's okay if they decide to explore and play instead. It's all about the experience! Continue whisking as much as your child likes and talk about what's happening to the soap.

END: When finished, show your child how to pour the water into the sink and wipe down all the materials with the cloth. Return the materials to the tray and place it back where you got it for next time.

Try this! This is a great activity for the bath or outdoors.

36. Window Polishing

TARGET SKILL: INDEPENDENCE
TODDLER AGE: 2 TO 3
PREP TIME: 1 TO 5 MINUTES

Busy toddlers love moving their bodies! In Montessori, we give them purposeful activities that help burn energy, and window washing is a favorite.

MATERIALS:

- ☐ Small spray bottle
- ☐ Water
- ☐ White vinegar
- ☐ Child-size cloth
- ☐ Small, divided caddy

PREP: Fill the spray bottle with a small amount of water-and-vinegar mixture (2 parts water to 1 part vinegar). Place the bottle and cloth in the caddy and on the child's shelf.

BEGINNING: Show the caddy to your toddler and tell them it's for making windows sparkle! Model how to carry the caddy over to a window of their choice and set it on the floor. Name each item in the caddy and remove the spray bottle. Give the window a gentle spray. Show your toddler how to wipe it with the cloth.

MIDDLE: Now it's their turn! Observe to see if they need help spraying the correct amount. If they don't get all the drips, that's okay! It takes practice. They can move around to multiple windows for as long as they like, taking the caddy with them.

END: When your toddler is finished, model how to return the caddy to the shelf in their prepared space.

Try this! This is another great activity to try outside, especially on a hot day.

Use this! A basket can also work if you don't have a caddy.

Psychological studies
have shown that it is
necessary to isolate the
senses as far as possible
if some single quality is to
be brought out.

—DR. MARIA MONTESSORI

CHAPTER 6

THE FIVE SENSES: ACTIVITIES FOR SENSORY STIMULATION

The Montessori sensorial activities are some of the most beautiful in a child's prepared environment! They are also some of the easiest to create at home. Your toddler's entire world is a sensorial experience.

In Montessori, the sensorial activities are developmentally foundational for a child. They provide pre-math skills, such as color grading and learning qualitative and quantitative words like hard and soft, heavy to light, biggest to smallest, and longest to shortest. The Montessori Method places such an importance on strengthening a child's senses because it builds concentration and independence. It also helps a child slow down and truly observe their environment.

Nature provides all your child's needs to strengthen their sensorial experience. Some activities in this chapter help get you and your child outside and exploring nature, such as the first activity, so let's begin!

37. Listening Walk: Nature Sound Games

TARGET SKILL: AUDITORY MEMORY
TODDLER AGE: 1 TO 3
PREP TIME: 1 TO 5 MINUTES

The outdoors offers endless sensorial possibilities. A favorite game of mine is a listening walk. It's a chance for you and your toddler to explore nature while listening to and identifying sounds, which refines their auditory sense.

MATERIALS:

☐ Weather-appropriate clothing for you and your toddler

PREP: Choose a safe location in nature where your child can explore.

BEGINNING: Arrive at your location and tell your child you are going on a listening walk. Explain that you'll be exploring and listening for different sounds. Set off on your adventure!

MIDDLE: In the Montessori Method, we move at the child's pace. Toddlers love to stop and explore. Give them the opportunity to do that, and draw their attention to sounds that you hear. You might hear a bird call, an insect chirping, or even just the wind. This game is about slowing down and being mindful of your surroundings. Ask your toddler if they hear the sound, too. With practice, they will begin to identify sounds themselves!

END: On the way home, revisit some of the sounds you heard, saying, "I remember hearing a bird." Then try mimicking the sound.

Try this! Even in the city, there are lots of interesting sounds! This game works perfectly in an urban environment.

38. Montessori Shape Recognition

TARGET SKILL: VISUAL DISCRIMINATION
TODDLER AGE: 1 TO 3
PREP TIME: 1 TO 5 MINUTES

This is a favorite in Montessori toddler classrooms, and you can use it at home with your toddler, too! It refines the visual sense while building pre-math vocabulary and problem-solving skills.

MATERIALS:

☐ Wooden knob puzzle with triangle, square, and circle shapes

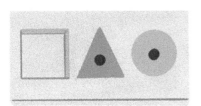

PREP: Place the puzzle on a shelf in the prepared environment.

BEGINNING: Invite your toddler to the shelf to see the puzzle, and model how to bring it to a worktable or mat. When your toddler is seated, model how to remove each of the shapes and name them as you go. Place each shape on the surface directly in front of the hole you removed it from. Ask your child to move their fingers around the sides of the hole. This helps make a sensorial impression in their brain.

MIDDLE: Invite them to pick up the circle and return it to its hole. Your toddler may not pick it up by the peg, and that's okay! Let them try to get each shape back into its place independently. If they succeed, make positive statements such as, "All the shapes are back in place!" instead of "Good job!" or "Good boy/girl!"

END: When your toddler is finished, model returning the puzzle to the shelf.

Try this! This is an easy DIY with cardboard, a sharp knife, and three different-colored felt markers!

39. Long, Longer, Longest

TARGET SKILL: GRADING SIMILAR OBJECTS
TODDLER AGE: 1 TO 3
PREP TIME: 5 MINUTES

This Montessori activity helps toddlers refine their visual sense and find small differences in similar objects.

MATERIALS:

☐ 3 to 5 sticks of similar circumference, but varying length
☐ Basket

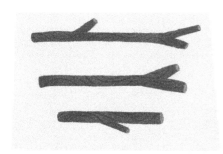

PREP: Arrange the sticks in a basket and place it on your child's shelf.

BEGINNING: Show the basket to your toddler and invite them to bring it to a worktable or mat. Model how to remove the twigs and lay each on the mat. Identify the shortest stick and place it on the mat. Ask your child to find the next longest. Don't correct them if it's not right, just keep going.

MIDDLE: When all sticks are lined up on the mat, ask your child to pass you the shortest one. Observe their reaction. Ask them to pass you the next longest and so on until they've handed you all the sticks. The focus is on the vocabulary association, so it's okay if they don't get all the sticks in the right order. It will take some practice.

END: When your toddler is finished, place all the sticks back in the basket and return it to the shelf.

Use this! Use items from around the house, like different-length pieces of paper (all the same color), if you can't find sticks.

Try this! Add more objects as your child practices!

40. Montessori Nature Tower

TARGET SKILL: GRADING SIMILAR OBJECTS
TODDLER AGE: 1 TO 3
PREP TIME: 5 TO 10 MINUTES

This outdoor activity helps toddlers recognize qualitive differences, the important first steps in math!

MATERIALS:

☐ 3 to 5 round stones of varying size, suitable for stacking

PREP: Collect the stones and group them in a pile at a prepared outdoor area.

BEGINNING: Talk to your toddler about the pile of stones you've collected. Your toddler can explore them and feel if they are rough or smooth, heavy or light. Now tell them you are going to start a stacking game! Ask them to give you the biggest stone. Then ask them to give you the next biggest. It's okay if they don't get this right away. Allow them to explore and bring their focus back to the stacking of the stones.

MIDDLE: Model how to stack the stones carefully from the biggest stone on the bottom to the smallest stone on the top. Then name each, starting at the top, by saying, "Big, bigger, bigger, biggest!" Allow your toddler to have a try and encourage them to use the same sensorial language.

END: When your toddler is finished, you can choose to leave the stones there in nature or bring them home to continue this activity.

Use this! Can't get outside? There are many beautiful stacking toys available, or you can make your own from cardboard.

41. Animal Sound Matching

TARGET SKILL: AUDITORY MEMORY
TODDLER AGE: 1½ TO 3
PREP TIME: 5 TO 10 MINUTES

Matching animal sounds to animal figurines is a great way to expand your child's abstract thinking and strengthen their auditory sense.

MATERIALS:

☐ Audio recordings of matching animal sounds
☐ 5 animal figurines your child knows well
☐ Basket

PREP: Prepare the sound recordings so they are readily accessible, place the animal figurines in the basket, and place the basket on a shelf.

BEGINNING: Invite your child to the shelf and show them the prepared activity. Model how to bring it to a worktable or mat. Remove the figurines from the basket and name each one. Tell your toddler you are going to play some animal sounds. Play one sound at a time and identify each sound.

MIDDLE: Now it's your child's turn! Play the first sound and ask, "What animal did you hear?" Ideally, they'll pick up the correct figurine. If not, that's okay! This takes some practice. Continue until all the sounds have been played. You can also try imitating the sounds yourself! Have fun exploring each of the different animal sounds and making your voice higher or deeper.

END: When your toddler is finished, return all the animals to the basket and ask your child to place it back on the shelf.

Try this! Try using more animals or grouping them by theme, like birds, or by continent, such as African animals.

42. Nature Sensory Tray or Table

TARGET SKILL: SENSORY REFINEMENT
TODDLER AGE: 1½ TO 3
PREP TIME: 1 TO 5 MINUTES

A nature table is an important part of a Montessori prepared environment. It adds organic elements to the space and allows toddlers to use their senses more deeply to explore natural objects.

MATERIALS:

☐ Found objects from nature, such as feathers, twigs, stones, etc.
☐ Wooden tray with handles
☐ Nature images to display

❨Caution❩
Ensure that each item is safe for your child.

PREP: Arrange the nature objects on a tray or shelf in an interesting way. Place the images near the objects for your child to see.

BEGINNING: Invite your child to the space and show them the items. Name them and talk about a sensorial quality, such as how soft a feather is or how bumpy a twig is.

MIDDLE: Invite your toddler to touch and smell each of the objects. Allow them to explore! They can continue talking about the items or simply explore them quietly. You can talk with your toddler about the places these objects were gathered or help them make the connection between the images you've displayed and each object.

END: When finished, your toddler can replace the objects on the shelf or tray, arranging them how they like best. They can come back to this activity whenever they like.

Try this! Rotate the items in this space to keep your toddler's interest high.

43. Montessori Mystery Bags

TARGET SKILL: REFINING TACTILE SENSE
TODDLER AGE: 2 TO 3
PREP TIME: 5 MINUTES

Montessori mystery bags are one of my favorite games! They strengthen both tactile sense and vocabulary, too.

MATERIALS:

- ☐ Small familiar objects, such as animal figurines and nature items
- ☐ Cloth bag
- ☐ Basket or tray

›Caution‹
Supervision is required.

PREP: Place the figurines or nature items inside the cloth bag. Place the bag inside the basket and put it on the shelf.

BEGINNING: Show your child the bag and tell them you're going to play a game! Invite them to a work-table or mat. Remove each item from the bag and name it. Then show your child how to put all the items back in the bag and tell them you're ready to begin!

MIDDLE: Reach into the bag. Tell your toddler what you feel, such as, "I feel something soft and round" before bringing it out. Next, it's their turn! They can reach in, find an item, and give it a sensorial description. Then you can guess what it is.

END: Keep playing for as long as your toddler likes. When finished, return all the items to the bag, replace the bag in the basket, and invite your child to return it to the shelf.

Try this! Try putting duplicate items in two bags and ask them to use two hands to find identical objects!

44. Kinetic Sand Play

Kinetic Sand is a soft sand that holds its shape. It provides excellent sensorial experiences and language-building opportunities for a toddler.

MATERIALS:

- ☐ 2 cups Kinetic Sand
- ☐ Cookie cutters
- ☐ Butter knife
- ☐ Wooden tray with handles

⟩Caution⟨
Supervision is required.

PREP: Gather all the items on the wooden tray and place it on a shelf.

BEGINNING: Show your child the prepared tray and invite them to bring it to a worktable. Name the Kinetic Sand and model how to pick it up gently. Show your toddler the different ways you can use the cookie cutters and knife to work with the sand. Offer them new vocabulary by describing the sand.

MIDDLE: It's your toddler's turn! Observe as they pick up and use the sand in any way they like, as long as it's safe. They may need guidance to keep the sand in the tray or help using the knife. Allow them to work as independently as possible and for as long as they like.

END: When your toddler is finished, replace all the items back on the tray. Model how to sweep up any sand on the floor or table. Ask your toddler to return the tray to the shelf.

Try this! Try using other items that your toddler enjoys, such as toy vehicles, animals, or people figurines, with the sand.

45. DIY Color Matching

TARGET SKILL: VISUAL DISCRIMINATION
TODDLER AGE: 2 TO 3
PREP TIME: 5 TO 10 MINUTES

Montessori color tablets are a favorite material that invite a child to strengthen their visual sense. This easy-to-DIY home version helps build visual discrimination skills for your toddler!

MATERIALS:

☐ Large-circle craft punch
☐ Free paint chips
☐ Small container
☐ Wooden tray

PREP: Use the craft punch to make a hole in each paint chip. Save the cutouts and place them in the container. Arrange all the materials on the tray and place it on a shelf.

BEGINNING: Show your child the prepared tray and invite them to carry it to a worktable or mat. Remove the paint chips with holes and arrange them. Pick up a circular cutout and tell your child you are going to try to match it. They may suggest the answer! If so, ask if they would like a turn.

MIDDLE: Your toddler can take a cutout and match it to the correct paint chip. If they don't get it right, that's okay! Don't necessarily correct them in the moment. Observe and see if they correct it. If not, make an observation to start with that color next time.

END: When finished, return all the materials to the tray and replace the tray on the shelf.

Try this! When your child has become good at this game, try paint chips of the same color but different shades!

46. Fabric Basket

TARGET SKILL: TACTILE DISCRIMINATION
TODDLER AGE: 2 TO 3
PREP TIME: 5 TO 10 MINUTES

This activity draws a child to concentrate and focus on their tactile sense. It can be very calming!

MATERIALS:

- ☐ Small fabric squares in various textures (2 of each fabric)
- ☐ Basket

PREP: Cut matching squares of fabric and arrange them in the basket. Place the basket on a shelf.

BEGINNING: Invite your toddler to come and play a game! Model bringing the basket to the worktable and removing each pair of matching fabric squares. Ask your toddler to feel each square and help them name the texture, such as rough, soft, or smooth. Line up one set of squares on the table and replace all the second squares in the basket. Now we are ready to begin! Reach into the basket and pull out a square, feel it, and name the texture. Model matching it to the correct square in the lineup.

MIDDLE: Now it's your toddler's turn to try! They can get a square from the basket and match it to its mate. It's okay if they don't get it right away! Help them give some tactile description to their square, such as, "It's soft." They can continue matching squares or simply explore the different textures of the fabrics.

END: When your toddler is finished, model returning all the squares to the basket and replacing it on the shelf.

Use this! Old clothes are great to cut your squares from!

47. Sensory Fun in the Kitchen

TARGET SKILL: GUSTATORY SENSE REFINEMENT
TODDLER AGE: 2 TO 3
PREP TIME: 5 TO 10 MINUTES

Toddlers don't always like trying new foods. This is a great activity to help them explore new tastes!

MATERIALS:

- ☐ 4 different tastes: salty, sweet, sour, and bitter
- ☐ 4 small bowls
- ☐ 4 spoons
- ☐ Child-size cloth

⟩Caution⟨
Be aware of your child's food allergies.

PREP: Prepare each taste in a bowl, ideally some foods your child knows. Sweet could be sugar water. Bitter could be a green vegetable, sour could be lemon juice. Salty could be a small amount of salt in water. Arrange the items neatly on a tray in the prepared environment.

BEGINNING: Bring your child to where you've prepared this activity. Tell them you are going to try something new! Show them each of the bowls and ask them which one they want to try first, without telling them the taste.

MIDDLE: Put a small amount of the taste on the spoon for them to try. Observe their reaction! If your toddler is hesitant, you can always try the taste first and then name it. If they've tried multiple bowls, ask which is their favorite.

END: When finished, model how to wipe any spills with the cloth and ask your child to help, too. The bowls can be put in an area to be washed, or your toddler may enjoy washing them!

Try this! This activity can easily be done during a meal!

48. Smelling Jars

TARGET SKILL: STRENGTHENING OLFACTORY SENSE
TODDLER AGE: 2 TO 3
PREP TIME: 10 TO 15 MINUTES

Montessori smelling jars help a child focus their sense of smell in a controlled yet fun way! Starting with familiar scents works best.

MATERIALS:

- ☐ Scent for each jar
- ☐ Cotton balls (optional)
- ☐ 4 to 6 spice jars with perforated lids
- ☐ Wooden tray with handles

PREP: Add 1 scent, such as lemon, mint, or lavender, to 2 jars to make matching pairs of scents. If you're using essential oils, spray some on a cotton ball and put it in the jar. Cover the jars and arrange them neatly on a tray in the prepared environment, so it's inviting to your child.

BEGINNING: Show your child the tray and model carefully carrying it to a worktable or mat. Model how to carefully smell each jar and place the jars together when you find a matching scent.

MIDDLE: Your toddler can now try! Observe their reactions and allow them to work at their own pace. Use vocabulary with them, such as, "This scent is strong!" to keep the game Montessori focused. They may not make the matches correctly, and that's okay! Montessori is all about the experience.

END: Replace the lids on the jars and place them on the tray, then ask your toddler to return it to the shelf.

Try this! I love switching scents for the different seasons with this activity.

Children pass through a
period in which they can only
pronounce syllables; then they
pronounce whole words, and
finally, they use to perfection all
the rules of syntax and grammar.

—DR. MARIA MONTESSORI

CHAPTER 7

FUN WITH LANGUAGE: ACTIVITIES FOR LANGUAGE DEVELOPMENT

Language development begins at 18 weeks after conception, when an unborn child begins to hear. By the age of 1, there are so many fun and easy activities that can help your toddler build language and literacy skills!

Montessori focuses on a few key aspects regarding language. Sounds are taught before symbols, so we start by listening and talking! Visual discrimination comes next, and we use exciting sorting and matching games like the ones in this chapter. This leads to classification games, such as the sequencing and naming ones you'll find here.

Introducing easy-to-use activities that bring new language and literacy concepts to your toddler helps them make and strengthen the language centers of their developing brain. Just like in the other areas of development, language concepts are built sequentially, first meeting your child at their unique stage of development and building their confidence and independence from there.

49. Object Matching

TARGET SKILL: VISUAL DISCRIMINATION
TODDLER AGE: 1 TO 2
PREP TIME: 1 TO 5 MINUTES

This activity draws on a toddler's Sensitive Period for Small Objects and helps expand their vocabulary.

MATERIALS:

☐ 4 or 5 animal figurines
☐ 4 or 5 matching photographic cards or printouts
☐ Basket

PREP: Gather the figurines and cards in the basket and place it on the shelf.

BEGINNING: Show your toddler the activity and ask them to carry the basket to a mat. Model how to carefully remove each animal from the basket and name it before lining them up horizontally on the mat. Bring out one card at a time from the basket and show your child. Name the animal on the card and ask them to match it to the animal figurine. Then it's their turn!

MIDDLE: You can alter this game by having different figurines of the same animal (with cards to match), such as different dog breeds or birds. Observe and make notes of the words your child struggled with so you can alter this game to fit their needs.

END: When your toddler is finished, they can place all the animals and cards back in the basket and carefully carry it back to their shelf.

Try this! There are so many other items to build language with. If your toddler loves trucks or different foods, try these, too! Challenge your child by replacing the figures with matching card pairs.

50. Reading: More Than Just Story Time

TARGET SKILL: LITERACY SKILLS
TODDLER AGE: 1 TO 3
PREP TIME: 5 MINUTES

Reading to your child is one of the best things you can do to strengthen literacy skills and cognitive development! Here, we'll use some Montessori-compatible techniques for expanding the reading experience.

MATERIALS:

- ☐ Realistic picture books
- ☐ Matching figurines featured in the book, such as cats, dogs, and humans
- ☐ Basket
- ☐ Tray

PREP: Choose a realistic book for which you have matching figurines, such as a story about a cat. Gather the figurines in the basket on the tray and place it on a shelf. Stand the book next to the tray.

BEGINNING: Show your child the prepared activity and invite them to a comfortable space. Show them the figurines in the basket and tell them you are going to read the story but in a new way! Open the book and begin reading. Take some of the figurines and use them to act out what's happening in the story. Montessori encourages the use of expressive language, so experiment and have fun! Make voices for the people or different sounds for the animals!

MIDDLE: Encourage your child to try. They can move the figurines while you tell the story, or they can tell the story to you.

END: When your toddler is finished, return everything to the tray and replace it on the shelf.

Use this! Don't have a book with matching figurines? Make your own verbal story instead!

51. Parts of an Animal

TARGET SKILL: CLASSIFICATION
TODDLER AGE: 1 TO 3
PREP TIME: 1 TO 3 MINUTES

The Sensitive Period for Order is the perfect time to help toddlers build their classification and visual discrimination skills. This fun animal activity does just that!

MATERIALS:

☐ Large pictures of familiar animals, such as dogs, cats, or farm animals
☐ Wooden tray

PREP: Gather all the pictures on a tray and place it on your toddler's shelf.

BEGINNING: Show your child the activity and invite them to carry it to a worktable or mat. Lay out all the pictures and describe each one. "This is a black dog" or "This is an orange cat" are easy ways to begin this game. Choose a picture, point to the eyes, and name them. Then ask your toddler where the mouth is. If they don't point to the mouth, that's okay! Show them where it is and keep going. They will understand with practice.

MIDDLE: Continue asking your child where some of the body parts are on each of the animals. You can stick to faces if that's easiest! Some toddlers love comparing, so they may want to look at two pictures at a time to compare the eyes or nose. Observe and follow their interests.

END: Return everything to the tray and invite your toddler to replace it when finished.

Try this! Try arctic or jungle animals with your child, too!

52. Montessori Sorting Tray

TARGET SKILL: VISUAL DISCRIMINATION
TODDLER AGE: 1½ TO 3
PREP TIME: 5 MINUTES

Toddlers are in their Sensitive Period for Order, and this is the perfect time to introduce sorting. In Montessori, we do this to strengthen concentration, pre-reading, and visual discrimination skills.

MATERIALS:

- ☐ Sets of small miniatures, such as animals, rocks, or toys
- ☐ Small bowl
- ☐ Sectioned tray or basket

꙳Caution꙳
Supervision is required.

PREP: Gather all the objects in the small bowl, mixed together, and place the bowl in the basket on a shelf.

BEGINNING: Invite your child to come and see the new activity. Tell them it's a sorting game and model how to carry it to a worktable. Show them one of each set of objects and name it. Model how to carefully pick it up from the bowl and place it in one section of the tray or basket. Continue until you have one of each of the sets in a different section of the tray. Now invite your toddler to try!

MIDDLE: Your toddler can try matching each object to its set in the basket. This is a great way to strengthen concentration and the finger movements needed for writing later.

END: When your toddler is finished, show them how to return all the miniatures to the bowl and return this activity to the shelf.

Try this! Try using tongs to transfer the objects for some extra fine motor skill practice!

53. Pattern Fun

TARGET SKILL: SEQUENCING CONCEPTS
TODDLER AGE: 2 TO 3
PREP TIME: 5 MINUTES

Detecting and predicting patterns is essential for reading. Montessori presents these skills in a fun and easy-to-understand way to strengthen a toddler's critical thinking.

MATERIALS:

☐ Bingo daubers or dot markers in red, blue, and yellow
☐ Sheet of paper
☐ Plastic tray

PREP: Gather all the materials on the tray and place it on your toddler's shelf.

BEGINNING: Show your toddler the tray, telling them you're going to do a fun color game! Invite them to carry it to a worktable. Remove everything from the tray and tell your toddler you're going to try some patterns. Take the red dauber and make a mark on the blank sheet of paper. Next, make a blue mark to the right of the red, then make another red mark. The pattern is forming, and your toddler may already be able to see it!

MIDDLE: Observe to see if your toddler is noticing the pattern forming. Sometimes it helps to say the pattern: "I see red, blue, red, what goes next?" They can try stamping the pattern themselves or make new ones!

END: When finished, return all the materials to the tray and place it back on the shelf.

Try this! Ready for the next level? Try expanding the pattern to include three or more colors!

Use this! No daubers or dot markers? Try finger-painting a pattern!

54. Land, Air, and Water Game

TARGET SKILL: CLASSIFICATION
TODDLER AGE: 2 TO 3
PREP TIME: 5 TO 10 MINUTES

Toddlers love to classify different objects, and this activity expands their reasoning skills.

MATERIALS:

- ☐ Animal figures that include land, water, and flying animals
- ☐ Felt or fabric in light blue, green, and dark blue, or a land/air/water mat
- ☐ Small bowl for animals
- ☐ Tray

PREP: Gather all the materials on the tray and put it on your toddler's shelf.

BEGINNING: Invite your child to carry the tray to a worktable or mat. Remove the animals from the basket and tell your toddler you are going to play a game. Explain what each color of felt or section of the mat represents: dark blue water, green earth, light blue sky. Pick up an animal, ask what it is, then place it on the felt or mat in the correct place. It's your toddler's turn to try! Ask them to name the animal they pick up and then ask them where it lives.

MIDDLE: Observe your child as they place each animal in its correct place. If they make a mistake, that's okay! In Montessori, we don't correct a child in the moment. Instead, make a note of the gap in understanding and present this information at a later point.

END: When your toddler is finished, return everything back to the tray and ask them to carry it to the shelf.

Try this! If your child is ready, try expanding on this by using vehicles instead!

55. Emotion Cards

TARGET SKILL: LANGUAGE DEVELOPMENT
TODDLER AGE: 2 TO 3
PREP TIME: 1 TO 5 MINUTES

In Montessori, teaching emotional intelligence early is so important, and these cards help make a fun game for toddlers!

MATERIALS:

- ☐ Printed pictures of faces with different expressions
- ☐ Small basket
- ☐ Small mirror
- ☐ Wooden tray

PREP: Prepare the pictures of people and place them in the small basket. Gather all the materials on a tray and place it on the shelf.

BEGINNING: Show the tray to your toddler and invite them to bring it to a worktable. Remove one card and describe the facial emotion to your child. "Look at this child, see their smile? They look happy!" Place the card on the table. Pick up the mirror and model how to make a happy face in the mirror for your toddler.

MIDDLE: Time for your child to try! Pick up another card and describe the emotion on it. You can tell your child, "Look at this child, see their frown and tears? They look sad." Model how to make each expression in the mirror and match it to each card. When all the cards are on the table, pick up each one, and ask your child to identify the emotion.

END: Replace everything on the tray and invite your child to return it to the shelf.

Try this! Begin with happy, sad, and mad, then add more emotions as you go!

56. Montessori I Spy Game

TARGET SKILL: PHONETIC AWARENESS
TODDLER AGE: 2 TO 3
PREP TIME: 1 TO 5 MINUTES

This favorite classroom activity is so easy to play at home, too! It builds phonetic awareness, which is the basis of reading.

MATERIALS:

- ☐ Cat, dog, and pig figurines
- ☐ Basket

PREP: Place the animal figurines in a basket on your child's shelf.

BEGINNING: Tell your child you have a special game to play and invite them to carry the basket to a worktable or mat. Remove the animals from the basket, naming each animal and placing them in a horizontal line. Now you're ready! Say to your toddler, "I spy with my little eye something that starts with a c," making the phonetic sound of the letter. Your toddler can pick up the cat. If they don't, that's okay! Go back over each of the animal names, stressing the first letter's sound.

MIDDLE: Move on to each animal, saying, "I spy with my little eye something that starts with" and then making the phonetic sound. Follow the child and observe. They may struggle with some of the sounds, and that's okay! Keep practicing.

END: When finished, place everything back in the basket and invite your toddler to return it to the shelf.

Try this! You can play this outside, too! Choose something you see and begin the game.

57. Sequence Card Games: Morning Routine

TARGET SKILL: VISUAL DISCRIMINATION
TODDLER AGE: 2½ TO 3
PREP TIME: 5 TO 10 MINUTES

Sequencing is an important pre-reading and writing skill. In Montessori, we use card stories with toddlers to help this abstract concept become concrete.

MATERIALS:

☐ Sequence cards
☐ Basket

PREP: Print or draw sequence cards that, when placed in the correct order, represent a beginning, middle, and end. Place the cards in a basket on the shelf.

BEGINNING: Show your child the activity and invite them to bring it to a worktable or mat. Take out each of the three cards and describe them, then mix them up to begin! Choose the first card in the sequence. Perhaps it's a child sleeping in their bed. Place it to the left on the work surface. Choose the next card and show your toddler. Perhaps it has the child waking up and leaving their bed. Place it next to the first card. Model sorting the cards with your toddler, talking about what is happening in each picture.

MIDDLE: Your toddler can work with this material as long as they like. If they are struggling to sequence the cards, remove some so it becomes more obvious. Feel free to make up a story about what's happening in the pictures!

END: When your toddler is finished, return the materials to the storage basket and place it on the shelf.

Try this! Try other sequences, such as the seasons or getting dressed.

58. Rhyming Games

TARGET SKILL: PHONETIC AWARENESS
TODDLER AGE: 2½ TO 3
PREP TIME: 5 TO 10 MINUTES

Rhyming is an important component of the Montessori pre-reading curriculum because it builds phonetic awareness and word association skills. We use the child's Sensitive Period for Small Objects to further these skills in fun, child-led games!

MATERIALS:

☐ Miniature toys in rhyming pairs, such as cat/hat, dog/log, and bug/rug
☐ Basket

PREP: Place the miniature toys in a basket on the shelf.

BEGINNING: Show your child the activity and invite them to bring it to a worktable or mat. Take the items out one at a time, name each item, and line them up horizontally. Begin by pointing to the cat and saying, "This is a cat. I can find something that rhymes. Look, a hat!" Pick up both items and place them in a pair, saying each item's name again.

MIDDLE: It's your child's turn! Go back over the names of the items. In Montessori, we use as much verbal language as we can. Observe to see if your toddler needs some clues. Help only when necessary and try to limit phrases like "good job."

END: When your toddler is finished, return the items to the basket and replace it on the shelf.

Use this! Try using pictures of objects if you don't have miniatures.

Try this! You can try this game when outside with your toddler, too!

59. Montessori Sand Tray

TARGET SKILL: FINE MOTOR SKILLS
TODDLER AGE: 2½ TO 3
PREP TIME: 1 TO 5 MINUTES

This favorite of the Montessori classroom is a great way to build finger strength and muscle memory in toddlers. Toddlers love the repetition, too!

MATERIALS:

☐ Writing medium (sand, salt, or cornmeal work well)
☐ Wooden tray with handles

PREP: Pour writing medium in the tray and shake it to make an even layer of the medium. Place the tray on a shelf.

BEGINNING: Invite your toddler to the shelf and show them the tray. Tell them you are going to make some fun shapes and ask them to carry it to a worktable. Tell your child what material is in the tray. Show them how to point their index finger and draw a line in the loose material. You can draw a wavy line or shapes like a circle. Gently shake the tray when finished to level the material and "erase" your drawing. Now it's your toddler's turn!

MIDDLE: This is an excellent opportunity for you to observe your child's movements. Note which types of marks they are most curious about. Do they make Xs or circles? Do they enjoy shaking the tray to make the material level?

END: When finished, return the tray to the shelf. Invite your child to sweep the area if necessary.

Try this! You can invite your toddler to make the first letter of their name in lowercase.

60. Montessori Sandpaper Letters

TARGET SKILL: FINE MOTOR SKILLS
TODDLER AGE: 2½ TO 3
PREP TIME: 5 TO 10 MINUTES

This classic Montessori material, made out of boards with letters cut out of sandpaper, builds muscle memory and pre-writing skills that are essential for reading and writing.

MATERIALS:

☐ 5 sandpaper letters
☐ 5 small figurines or other small items
☐ Basket
☐ Tray

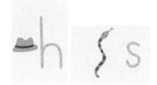

PREP: Pick any 5 sandpaper letters and pair each with a figurine or other small item that has the same beginning sound. Place everything in the basket on the shelf.

BEGINNING: Show your toddler the activity and invite them to carry it to a table. Remove all 5 objects and name them. Pull out one letter, place it on the table, and using your index and middle finger, trace around the rough letter while telling your child, "This makes the sound ___" (say the phonetic sound). Remember that Montessori teaches the letter sounds, not the letter names, at this stage. Then tell your child, "I spy something that starts with "__" and pick up the item and place it on the letter.

MIDDLE: Invite your child to try! Introduce them to the next letter and its sound and ask them to find the item with that beginning sound. Work through each of the sounds.

END: When your child is finished, replace the items on the tray and return it to the shelf.

Try this! DIY this activity with cardstock and sandpaper for an inexpensive home option.

RESOURCES

Want to know more about Montessori? Here are some of my favorite authentic resources from around the world!

WEBSITES

★ **Aid to Life,** *AidToLife.org*
A branch of the Association Montessori Internationale, this website is extremely helpful for finding practical information regarding Montessori and young children from 0 to 3 years old.

★ **American Montessori Society,** *AMSHQ.org/families/reading-material*
The American Montessori Society is the Montessori school and teacher accreditor in the United States and offers lots of great articles and resources for toddler caregivers.

★ **Our Montessori Life,** *OurMontessoriLife.com*
This is me! Our website offers families and schools Montessori-compatible book recommendations and shelf activities as well as nature study themes and child development information! I share what has worked for my family and in my many Montessori classrooms over the years.

BOOKS

★ *Understanding the Human Being: The Importance of the First Three Years of Life,* by Silvana Quattrocchi Montanaro
This book is a must for all of us in the Montessori infant/toddler world! Dr. Montanaro was a leader in her field, and this book gives so many eye-opening moments to caregivers.

★ *Montessori at Home: A Practical Guide for Parents,* by Tara Greaney
A practical guide for implementing the Montessori Method into your home life, from your child's birth to age 6, this book can help you meet your child's developmental needs at each age and stage.

REFERENCES

★ Montessori, Maria. *The Absorbent Mind.* Oxford, England: Clio Press, 1988.

★ Montessori, Maria. *The Child in the Family.* Oxford, England: Clio Press, 1989.

★ Montessori, Maria. *The Discovery of the Child.* Oxford, England: Clio Press, 1988.

★ Montessori, Maria. "Education and Peace: Address Given at 2nd International Montessori Congress, Nice, France, (1932)." *National Montessori Reporter* 7, no. 1 (1983): 5, 12.

★ Montessori, Maria. *Education for a New World.* Oxford, England: Clio Press, 1989.

★ Montessori, Maria. *From Childhood to Adolescence.* Oxford, England: Clio Press, 1996.

INDEX

Age 1

Maximum Effort: Walker
Wagon Push, 20

Age 1 to 2

Object Matching, 76

Age 1 to 3

Animal Rubber Stamps, 38
Baby Doll Bath, 54
Ball Games, 27
Beanbag Toss, 21
Bowling Games, 26
Cutting a Banana, 51
Helping with the Dishes, 50
Helping with the Laundry, 53
Hole Punching, 35
Hop, Skip, and Jump, 29
Listening Walk: Nature
Sound Games, 62
Long, Longer, Longest, 64
Montessori Coin Drop, 23
Montessori Glue Tray, 34
Montessori Jacket Flip, 48
Montessori Nature Tower, 65
Montessori Shape
Recognition, 63

Moving to Music, 22
Nature Suncatchers, 39
Open and Close Containers, 49
Parts of an Animal, 78
Plant Care, 52
Play Silks and Music, 24
Rainbow Hand Painting, 36
Reading: More Than Just
Story Time, 77
Sidewalk Chalk Design
and Erase, 37
Up, Up, Up: Climbing Fun, 28
Wheelbarrow Work:
Outdoor Fun, 25

Age 1½ to 3

Animal Sound Matching, 66
Introducing Scissors the
Montessori Way, 42
Lock Box Fun, 55
Montessori Sorting Tray, 79
Nature Sensory Tray or Table, 67
Play Dough Fun, 40
Sticker Fun, 41
Sweeping with Broom
and Dustpan, 56
Threading Beads, 43

Age 2 to 3

Color Mixing, 44
DIY Color Matching, 70
Emotion Cards, 82
Fabric Basket, 71
Juicing an Orange, 57
Kinetic Sand Play, 69
Land, Air, and Water Game, 81
Montessori I Spy Game, 83
Montessori Mystery Bags, 68
Pattern Fun, 80
Sensory Fun in the Kitchen, 72
Smelling Jars, 73
Toddler Animal Yoga, 31
Walking on the Line, 30
Whisking Bubbles, 58
Window Polishing, 59

Age 2½ to 3

Montessori Sandpaper
Letters, 87
Montessori Sand Tray, 86
Rhyming Games, 85
Sequence Card Games:
Morning Routine, 84
Toddler Collage Crafts, 45

ABOUT THE AUTHOR

BETH WOOD is a 0–3- and 3–6-year-old accredited Montessori teacher and a 6–12-year-old accredited Montessori Assistant. She is the owner of Our Montessori Life, a Montessori educational consulting agency that helps schools, families, and communities implement the peaceful, respectful, child-led principles of the Montessori Method into their days. Born in a small town in Ontario, and currently residing on the west coast of Vancouver Island, Canada, Beth has a love of nature and insatiable curiosity about the world that have fueled her Montessori work not only with her own two children, but also with many children around the world. For more about Beth, follow her on Instagram at @OurMontessoriLife and on Facebook at Facebook.com/ourmontessorilife.

ABOUT THE ILLUSTRATOR

DENISE HOLMES is a children's illustrator from Chicago, Illinois, where she lives with her husband and daughter. As a child, she loved to draw and knew she wanted to grow up to become an artist, so it was no surprise that she went on to become an illustrator. Today, Denise spends her time drawing and creating in her studio, and dreaming up new characters and the worlds they live in. Her work has been featured in books, magazines, and greeting cards. You can learn more about Denise on her website niseemade.com or follow her on Instagram @niseemade.

Printed in the USA
CPSIA information can be obtained
at www.ICGtesting.com
CBHW081005100524
8284CB00006B/55

9 781648 769207